HOW TO BE A BIG SISTER

HOW TO BE A BIG SISTER

A GUIDE TO BEING THE BEST OLDER SIBLING EVER

BY ASHLEY MOULTON

Illustrations by Kavel Rafferty

ROCKRIDGE
PRESS

For general information on our other products and services or to obtain technical support, please contact
our Customer Care Department within the United States at (866) 744-2665, or outside the United States
at (510) 253-0500.

Rockridge Press publishes its books in a variety of electronic and print formats. Some content that
appears in print may not be available in electronic books, and vice versa.

Interior and Cover Designers: Matt Girard and Tricia Jang
Art Producer: Meg Baggot
Editor: Erum Khan
Production Manager: Jose Olivera
Production Editor: Melissa Edeburn

Illustrations © Kavel Rafferty, 2020

ISBN: Print 978-1-64611-911-0
eBook 978-1-64611-912-7

R0

To Justin:
Thanks for making me an
expert big "stister."

Welcome to Big Sisterhood!

Dear Big Sister,

Congratulations! You are about to become even more awesome. Soon, you won't just be a regular old kid. You'll be a very special kind of kid . . . a big sister!

You might have a lot of questions about what that means, like: *Will the baby mess up all my stuff? When can we have dance parties together? Will my parent have less time for me?* Don't worry! This book is filled with advice from us, your fellow big sisters. We are girls just like you who have gone through this big change and are here to help.

Getting a new baby sibling is exciting. Because you're a big kid, you'll be able to help the baby. Before you know it, you will have a special friend to play with any time you want.

Being a big sister is really fun, but it also means that things are changing. You might have a lot of confusing feelings during this time (we all did!). That is totally normal. Your family will be different than it was before, and sometimes that can be hard. It's all part of growing up.

We can be *your* big sisters and tell you what becoming a sister might be like. Our families are all different, but we all have one thing in common: We are all big sisters.

By the time you're finished reading this book, you'll be ready to be the best big sister ever!

CHAPTER 1

BEFORE BABY ARRIVES

The time before a new baby arrives is so exciting! Your family will be busy getting ready, and everyone will be looking forward to meeting the newest family member. There are many ways you can start being a great big sister even before the baby comes.

Jada Goes to the Doctor

Jada got to see her baby sibling for the first time today . . . well, sort of! Jada's sibling was growing inside her mom's tummy. The only way to "see" the baby was through a special doctor's test called an ultrasound.

Jada went to the doctor's appointment with her mom. When they got there, the doctor squeezed a clear goo on her mom's stomach. The doctor touched the ultrasound wand to Jada's mom's tummy. This wand was kind of like magic. It showed a picture of the baby on a screen, even though the baby was still inside Jada's mom! The doctor moved the ultrasound wand around to see the baby from different angles and to make sure the baby was healthy.

The picture was pretty fuzzy, so Jada was not really sure what she was seeing until the doctor pointed to the outline of the baby's body. Jada put her hand on mom's tummy, and she could even feel the baby kick! Jada still had no idea what her sibling looked like, but she knew one thing: There was definitely a baby in there! She was so excited that she would meet the baby soon.

Libby Meets Someone New

It was a big day for Libby's family. It was their adoption home visit day! A social worker was coming to their house to meet Libby's family. A social worker is someone who helps families who want to adopt a child.

First, the social worker took a tour of the house. They needed to make sure that everything would be safe for a new baby. Then it was time for the social worker to ask Libby questions. It made Libby nervous. The social worker explained that Libby couldn't give any wrong answers, so that made Libby feel better. Most of the questions were easy to answer, like "How do you feel about having a new brother or sister?" (Excited!) and "What are your parents like?" (They love me very much!)

A few months passed while the adoption agency was finding a baby for Libby's family. One day, her parents got an exciting phone call. They had been matched with a baby girl and would get to bring her home in a few weeks. Libby was so excited she couldn't stand it! She looked at her new sister's picture every day while she waited to meet her.

What Can We Do Together?

Your family will be very busy getting ready for the new baby, and there's a lot you can do to help! Here are some ideas:

Make something special for the baby. Make something for the baby's space, like a painting, a toy, or a blanket.

Help set up the baby's space. Pick out art to hang on the wall, help your parent build the crib, and unpack gifts.

Get the baby's clothes ready. Pick out a special outfit the baby can wear during their first day home. Help sort hand-me-down clothes into different sizes. Hang tiny outfits in the closet. Decide which outfit you would like to wear if it came in your size!

Help pick the baby's name. Look through a baby name book or website with your parent, and write down your favorite names. Just for fun, also write down the silliest names you find.

Sing to the baby. Did you know that babies can hear things even before they are born? If you sing a special song over and over to your sibling, they might even recognize it once they are born!

What Do I Think?

Now that you've read this chapter, it's a great time to think about any questions you might have about becoming a big sister. We've written some questions to get you started, but you can add more. You can think about your answers, write them down, or talk about them with your family.

What am I most looking forward to when I become a big sister?

What makes me most nervous about becoming a big sister?

What will the baby be like? How will they act?

What things will our family need to do to get ready for the baby? How can I help?

CHAPTER 2

BECOMING A BIG SISTER

You're ready to become a big sister, and now the special day is here! There are many ways for a baby to join a family. No matter how it happens in your family, it will be a day you'll never forget.

Yasmin Visits Her Nana

Yasmin's parents woke her up and said, "Today you're going to meet your brother!" Yasmin's mom was going to the hospital to have her baby. Before her parents went to the hospital, they dropped her off at her grandmother's house.

Yasmin and her nana had fun baking cookies while they were waiting for her brother to be born. Finally, after what seemed like forever, they got an exciting phone call. Yasmin was officially a big sister!

Nana and Yasmin drove to the hospital, and a nurse told them which room to go to. Yasmin's mom was resting in a bed, and her teeny tiny brother was in a special baby bed next to her. To help Yasmin hold her brother, Nana put a pillow in Yasmin's lap and carefully placed her brother in Yasmin's arms. Yasmin couldn't believe he was finally here!

Sofia Stays Home

Sofia's mom was ready to have her baby, so she called the midwife and said it was time. A midwife is someone who helps people give birth.

The midwife came to their house and Sofia helped her bring her things inside. Sofia's mom was doing a lot of hard work because her body was getting ready to have the baby. To help her, Sofia brought her water to drink and rubbed her back.

After a while, the midwife said that it was time for the baby to come and asked Sofia to wait in her room. Sofia played by herself for a while. Then she heard a baby crying. The midwife brought Sofia back in the room, and she saw the baby lying on her mom's chest. She was so small and cute! Sofia walked over and gave her a big-sister kiss.

Christie Meets Her New Sibling

Christie's parents wanted to be foster parents. This meant that they wanted to be a temporary family for kids whose parents couldn't take care of them. When Christie's family signed up, they weren't sure when a foster child would come to live with them or how old the child would be. One day they got a phone call that a toddler would be coming to live with them in a few hours. They had to make a quick trip to the store to get clothes and supplies.

Christie was waiting nervously when she heard a knock at the door. When she and her parents answered it, they found a social worker holding the hand of her new foster brother. Christie waved hello and helped give him a tour of their house. She read her foster brother a book she had made for him all about their family. She hoped her new foster brother would like it here!

What Can We Do Together?

It can be hard waiting for a baby to arrive. Here are some things you can do to pass the time while you're waiting to meet your new sibling:

Make a welcome poster. Do you know the baby's name yet? Make a giant poster that says "Welcome home, (name)!" and hang it on the door to your house.

Make a book about your family. Help your sibling get to know your family by making a picture book about the people in your family, where you live, and things you like to do together. Draw your pictures on plain paper, punch holes on one side, and put the pages in a binder or tie it together with string.

Pick out a stuffed animal for the baby. Ask the grown-up that is waiting with you to help you pick out a new stuffed animal. You can also wash one of your stuffed animals to give to the baby.

Bake cookies. With a grown-up, make a batch of cookies for your parent. Your parent might be really tired, and delicious cookies will help cheer them up!

Make a flower bouquet. Flowers are a nice way to tell your parent "Congratulations!" Make a bouquet of paper flowers or flowers you picked from a garden (after asking permission).

What Do I Think?

You might have some questions about what will happen when your sibling joins your family. Here are some questions you might want to ask your family. You can write down your own, too.

What will happen the day I get a sibling?

How long will it take for me to meet the baby?

Who will be taking care of me while I'm waiting?

Where will I be while I'm waiting?

CHAPTER 3
YOU'RE A BIG SISTER!

Congratulations! You're a big sister now! Here's how you can be a super big sister for your brand-new sibling.

Nap Time

Babies sleep a lot! When they are first born, it will seem like your sibling is *always* sleeping. They even sleep during the day when you are wide awake.

After a few months, your sibling will stay awake for longer stretches during the day, but they will still need to take naps for a couple of years. This might be really annoying sometimes. Your family might have to stop what you're doing so your sibling can go home and take a nap. Try to remember that you are being an awesome big sister by helping your sibling get the sleep they need. Your sibling will also be less fussy when they get enough rest. You can use the quiet time to read, color, or play.

Super Safe Sister Tip

Always ask a grown-up before giving your sibling a blanket or a stuffed animal, especially when they are sleeping.

Feeding Baby

You might be excited to share some of your favorite foods with your sibling . . . but wait! They are only going to drink milk or formula for the first few months. They will start eating "solid food" eventually, but this food won't be very solid at all. Babies' first foods are soft because they are learning how to chew and swallow. Your sibling's first food might be something like mashed-up bananas or vegetables that have been blended smooth.

As they get older, they will learn how to eat different kinds of food. Soon you'll be able to eat the same yummy foods together!

Super Safe Sister Tip

Always ask a grown-up before giving a baby food or anything else they might put in their mouth.

Super Helper Sister Tip

It's hard for your parent to get up when they're feeding a small baby. You can take them things they need, like a drink of water or a clean burp cloth. Your parent might teach you how to feed your sibling. When your sibling starts eating food, you can help them learn to like new foods by smiling and saying "yummy" when they try something new.

Changing Baby's Diapers

All the milk the baby drinks has to go somewhere! Your sibling won't know how to use the potty for a long time. They will use diapers instead. Babies need to have their diapers changed often, sometimes 12 times a day!

Super Helper Sister Tip

You can help your parent by handing them a clean diaper or a wipe, or by throwing away the dirty diaper. Sing a song to your sibling to help keep them calm while being changed.

Bath Time

Your baby sibling is so tiny they might take their first baths in the sink. Since babies can't sit up on their own, your sibling might use a special baby bathtub to help them stay safe. You can be a bath-time buddy by playing a gentle game of "splish-splash" when they are in the tub, or by gently pouring water on their arms and legs. Just be careful not to get water on their face! When your sibling gets older and stronger, they will be able to take bubble baths in the tub just like you.

Super Safe Sister Tip
There should always be a grown-up around when your sibling is in the bath.

23

Adventure Time

When it's time to do fun stuff with your family, your sibling needs help to get around. If you all have to drive somewhere, they will get strapped into a car seat in the backseat. Some babies don't like this very much. If your sibling doesn't like their car seat, try singing songs or making funny faces to distract them.

When you're walking somewhere, your sibling will need help since they can't walk yet. Often, they will get pushed in a stroller. Your parent might also carry them in a special baby backpack.

Playtime

You *will* be able to play with your sibling when they're a little baby, but you won't be climbing on the monkey bars with them in the beginning. It can be surprising when a baby is born because they don't know how to do much besides eat and sleep.

There is a lot your sibling has to learn before they can play. First, they will learn how to follow something with their eyes. Then they will learn how to move their arms and legs on purpose. Finally, they will learn how to hold a toy in their hand. Soon, your sibling will be rolling, crawling, and walking. Great news, big sister: You can help them learn how to do all these things! Playing with your sibling might be very different from how *you* play, but it is still really fun.

Super Safe Sister Tip

Be very gentle when playing with your sibling. Always ask a grown-up before holding them or picking them up.

Babies LOVE putting everything in their mouths, and you can help them play safely. Small toys are not safe for babies, so ask a grown-up before giving them anything to play with. Once your sibling is able to move around on their own, make sure you keep your toys (like blocks, marbles, or doll accessories) away from them.

Yuki Plays Gently

At first, Yuki was disappointed when her newborn brother came home because he seemed pretty boring. But then she realized that she *could* play with her brother. She just had to play like a baby! Yuki made funny faces and noises at him every day. When he was two months old, he started to smile back at her. A few weeks later, she made him laugh for the first time. Because she was so silly, she could make him laugh even when her parents couldn't. Yuki felt proud of her special big sister silly power.

She wanted to teach her brother how to move his arms, so she asked her dad if she could hold things like rattles and stuffed animals near her brother's hands. One day, when he was three months old, she handed him a toy. To her amazement, he could hold it! It was fun watching him learn.

Naina Helps Baby Learn

Naina's dad told her how her baby sister needed to do lots of "tummy time" so that her neck would get stronger. Her dad placed her sister on her tummy on the floor. Naina got down next to her and shook a rattle. "Come on, baby, look up here!" she said to encourage her sister.

As Naina's sister got stronger, Naina's new goal was to teach her to roll over. She held a toy just out of her sister's reach, and her sister kicked her legs to try to turn over. It was cute to watch her try a new skill!

Emma Plays with Toys

Emma loved playing with her brother now that he could sit up by himself and hold toys. Emma's favorite thing to do was play peek-a-boo. She held up a blanket in front of her brother's face and said, "Where's Emma?" Then her brother pulled the blanket down and giggled when Emma said, "You found me!"

Emma liked sharing some of her toys with her brother, too. She built a tall block tower for her brother to knock over and tickled him with a puppet. Emma loved playing with her brother every day after school.

What Can We Do Together?

Draw black-and-white pictures. Newborns can't see very well, but one thing they can see is black-and-white pictures. Hold your pictures up in front of your sibling. They will probably want to stare at each picture for a minute or two!

Have a dance party. Put on your favorite music and dance around the room where your sibling can see you. With a grown-up's help, you can gently move the baby's arms and legs, or your parent can pick the baby up and dance around the room with them.

Read a book. Babies love hearing people's voices, so read your sibling a story! Your sibling won't understand how to pay attention to a book at first, but soon they'll learn to like them and will be excited to turn the pages.

Teach them new words. Point out everything you see and say the words out loud. You might say, "I see a tree. I see clouds. I see a car." Your sibling won't speak words until they are about one year old, but they start learning what words mean from the very beginning.

Be a bath-time buddy. Play a gentle game of "splish-splash" with your sibling when they are in the tub, or gently pour water on their arms and legs. Be careful not to get water on their face!

What Do I Think?

Now that your sibling is here, you might be wondering about a lot of different things. Here are some questions you might want to ask your family, or you can write your own.

What will change about our family's routine?

Is there a special job I can have to help with the baby?

When will things go back to normal?

When will the baby learn to (walk, talk, read...)?

CHAPTER 4

GROWING UP TOGETHER

Before you know it, your baby sibling won't be a baby anymore! Once your sibling is walking and talking, they will be able to join you on all sorts of adventures. They will become an awesome friend. There are so many things to look forward to as your sibling gets older.

Being a Role Model

Did you know that your little sibling wants to be just like you? They probably think that you are the coolest person around. You might not realize it, but your sibling is learning things from you every day. You can be a super big sister and a role model for your sibling by setting a good example and teaching them to share toys, brush their teeth, and try new foods.

You can give expert advice for every new thing that happens to your sibling. You can help them through scary things like going to kindergarten, visiting the doctor, or disagreeing with a friend. It's been a long time since your parent has done kid things like losing a tooth, so you will be able to give special advice.

We have good news: Being a role model isn't all hard work! You can also be an awesome sister *and* have fun by just doing things you love with your sibling. If you love art, you can color with them. If you love sports, you can play outside with them (and maybe even let them win sometimes!). Whatever your favorite thing is, your sibling will want to do it with you.

Family Time

We've been talking a lot about the baby in this book, but this book is also about someone just as important . . . you!

One thing is for sure: A new baby will take up a lot of your parent's time. Your parent might be really, really tired. They might not have as much patience. These changes might make you feel sad because you miss your mom or dad a little. You might feel jealous of your sibling and wish you got as much attention as they do. You might feel bored because you have to play by yourself sometimes. You might wonder if your parent loves you as much as they did before. (Pinky promise: They do! They love you *so* much!) You might even wish things could go back to how they were before. All big sisters have a lot of very strong feelings when they get a new sibling, and that's totally normal.

Becoming a big sister means a lot of changes, but everything will get easier after some time. It's important to talk with your parent about how it feels for you to be a big sister. They can't help you if they don't know what's bothering you.

You can also look forward to special time alone with your parent. You could play a board game while your sibling naps. Or you could go on a fun date, like a trip to the museum. There are some things that only big kids can do. You'll get to do them alone with your parent! Together with your parent, plan some activities that can be your special time together.

What Can We Do Together?

As your sibling gets older, here are just some of the things you'll be able to do together:

Have a family movie night. Pick a movie together, pop some popcorn, and pile cozy blankets and pillows in front of the screen.

Make food together. Find a recipe in a cookbook and make it together. (Always ask a grown-up to help.)

Go to a playground. Ask a grown-up to take you to the playground for a game of tag or hide-and-go-seek.

Have a pretend tea party. Wear dress-up clothes, gather all your stuffed animals, and make food out of clay. Don't forget to pour some pretend tea!

Go for a swim. Head to family swim time at a nearby pool. (Always ask a grown-up to take you.)

Have an indoor campout. Gather blankets and sheets and build a tent in your living room. Pretend you're camping, make shadow puppets with a flashlight, and go to bed in sleeping bags.

Make a craft. Gather craft supplies like glue, paper, pipe cleaners, Popsicle sticks, or whatever you have in your house. Make something to give to your grandparent, aunt, teacher, or each other!

What Do I Think?

There's a lot to think about as you get used to being a big sister. These are some questions we had when we became big sisters, but you can add your own, too. Think about your answers or write them down. If you want, talk about them with your family afterward.

How do I feel about being a big sister?

What ideas do I have for special things I want to do alone with my parent?

What am I most looking forward to doing with my sibling when they're older?

What advice do I want to make sure I tell my sibling?

BIG SISTERS UNITE!

Well, you've done it! You have become a big sister. The Big Sisters in this book are *so* glad that you are now a member of our special club. We hope that our stories have helped you learn different ways to be a super sister.

You helped your family get ready for your new sibling. You learned how to help take care of them. You've thought about all the fun things you'll be able to do together when you are both older. All you have to do now is enjoy time with your new sibling and keep growing up *together*.

Remember that if you ever need more advice, you can ask other big sisters (and brothers) in your own life. They might be friends at school, teachers, or even people in your own family, but there are big sisters all around you. Don't forget to ask them for help! And of course, your parent will always be there to answer questions, too.

Love,
    The Sisters

Acknowledgments

A sincere thank-you to the grown-up who bought this book for a kiddo in your life. It is an honor and a privilege to be a small part of this special time for your family.

Thanks to Susan Haynes, Erum Khan, and the entire team at Callisto Media for inviting me to be a part of this project.

Thanks to Amy Chase, Alice Truscott, and Callum Borchers for providing me with big-sibling wisdom. Thanks to Addie, Ben, Charlotte, Emma, and Hazel: I imagine I'm talking to you every time I write something for kids! Thanks for being my inspiration.

Thanks as always to my parents and Dan for supporting everything I do, and to Juniper for giving me some firsthand "how to care for a new baby" material. I love you.

About the Author

Ashley Moulton has spent the last decade working in children's media at companies like Nickelodeon and YouTube and at her kids' cooking company, Nomster Chef. She is the author of *Let's Party! Kids Cookbook*, a cookbook with fun party recipes for kids, which was published in 2019.

Ashley graduated from Stanford's Graduate School of Education with an M.A. in learning, design, and technology in 2015, and from Ithaca College as a Park Scholar with a B.S. in television-radio in 2009. She lives in Philadelphia with her husband and daughter and loves cooking, travel, yoga, home design, and painting. Find her at AshleyMoulton.com.

CPSIA information can be obtained
at www.ICGtesting.com
Printed in the USA
JSHW052353280920
8336JS00004B/18